Drizzle
and the Letter

By Mary Ostrowski

Illustrated by René Ramos

Meet Drip

Drip's smile lights up a room, and she shares her happiness with pretty much everyone. She can be shy and is kind of a perfectionist. I bet you're thinking to yourself, "But no one is perfect." I know, right?! We sure do get crazy ideas in our heads sometimes, don't we? And sometimes, this makes **Drip** timid to try new things because she's afraid she'll get it wrong.

Meet Drop

Drop is so much fun to be around! He will make you laugh out loud — and then cringe in the next minute.

Drop can be impulsive. I mean, sometimes he says things he instantly regrets or makes a not-so-good choice without even knowing why he did it! This makes him feel bad because he really is nice, and doesn't mean to hurt anyone.

Meet Drizzle

Drizzle is the friend you feel like you've known forever. He seems to get everything right, but **Drizzle** makes mistakes like everyone else. Sometimes he gets in trouble. But he's self-confident enough to know he can get through it — so he does. He helps his friends get through stuff too. His friends think, "I want to be like **Drizzle**." The truth is, they can be.

We all have Drizzle within us.

Hello My Friend!

Allow me to tell you the story of **Drizzle and the Letter**.

I love discovering reasons to be proud of kids. But when they do something difficult, and even a little bit scary, well – that makes my heart feel like singing! And what **Drizzle** did on this particular day was difficult *and* kind of scary. I learned a little something too.

Happy Reading,

Ms. Mary

It was Tuesday.

Drizzle listened as **Ms. Mary** gave instructions to the class for their group activity. "Today we will see the value of teamwork," she said.

Drizzle admitted later that he was kind of tired and didn't really feel like doing any work.

Perhaps that played a role in what happened next?

"The more you work together, the easier your job will be," **Ms. Mary** said. "You may begin!"

Drip instantly picked up the page of directions and started telling her group what to do. "Okay. I'll be the leader. **Drop**, you write down the answers, and **Drizzle**..."

"No, **Drip**! I don't want to do that!" **Drop** interrupted. He grabbed the paper from her hands.

"Stop it!" **Drip** demanded, holding onto the paper tightly.

"No! Let me see!" **Drop** said.

Drizzle watched while **Drip** and **Drop** both tugged on the paper. "Come on you guys," he sighed. "Let's just do this."

Drizzle reached for the paper. **Drip** and **Drop** pulled it away from him. So **Drizzle** grabbed the page and pulled.

Drip and **Drop** pulled back.

"Let me have it!" **Drizzle** pulled harder...

...and the page ripped into two pieces!

"DRIZZLE!!!"

Ms. Mary heard the noise and turned just in time to see **Drip** and **Drop** looking distressed while **Drizzle**, a look of frustration on his face, held the ripped piece of paper in his hands.

"**Drizzle**," she said. "What is going on? Please stop distracting your group and get started on your work."

"Huh? Whaaat??"

Can you imagine how **Drizzle** felt in that moment when his teacher scolded him?

Can you imagine **Drip** and **Drop**'s reactions?

MAKE A PREDICTION!

Before reading any more, make a prediction. What do you think is going to happen next? How do you think the story might end?

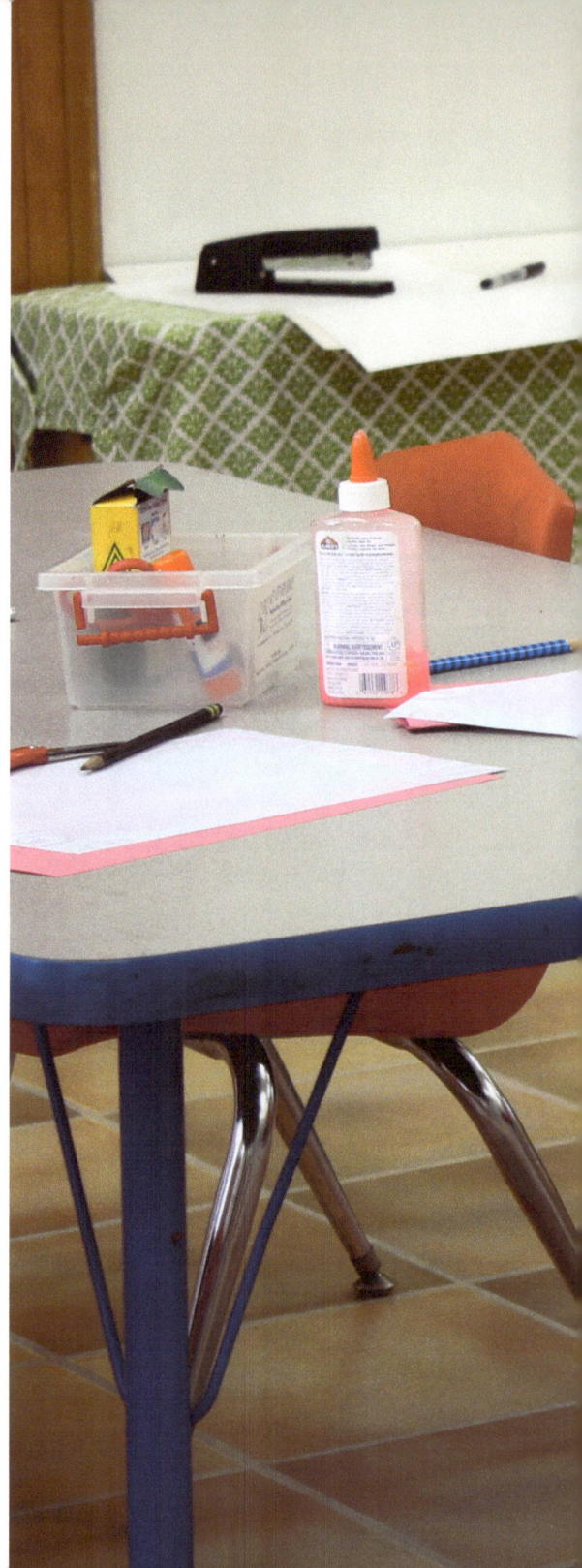

Drizzle looked at his teacher and cried, "Wait. What? It wasn't my fault!"

"**Drizzle**, please don't talk back to me," **Ms. Mary** replied. His friends were quiet.

Drizzle's face turned red. He looked at his friends and yelled, "You got me in trouble! I hate you!"

"**Drizzle**, that's enough. Go sit in the library and do a Raindrop Reflection to cool down."

> **RAINDROP REFLECTION**
>
> This worksheet helps children cool down by asking questions and encouraging them to write and draw.

Drizzle flopped down angrily in the library. He looked at the **Raindrop Reflection**. He pushed it away and put his head down.

> **MAKING CONNECTIONS**
>
> Pretend you are Drizzle. How are you feeling right now? Why?

Ms. Mary walked over to **Drizzle** saying, "You look mad right now, **Drizzle**. Take a few minutes to calm down. We all make poor choices at times, but they don't have to be the end of the world.

Use the **Raindrop Reflection** so we can talk. Be honest, and say what you need to say."

Then **Ms. Mary** walked away.

After a few minutes,
Drizzle began writing.

And writing.

And writing...

"Ms. Mary, I'm done." **Drizzle** looked nervous. He handed her his paper. She read it.

She read it again.

Ms. Mary looked at **Drizzle**.

Name: Drizzle

Raindrop Reflection

Hello my friend. What's bothering you? Take some time to think about the questions. When you're finished, let's talk about it.

How are you feeling?
Mad and sad

What is something you can do to help yourself feel more calm? Do it!
Some ideas: Take 10 deep breaths. Draw a picture. Write a letter.
Write a letter

What happened?
After you gave directions, Drip started telling me and Drop what to do. Drop got mad at her and grabbed the paper. She didn't like that and grabbed the paper back. They were so annoying. I just wanted to get finished! I grabbed the paper to read it, but they pulled it away from me. I pulled harder and then it ripped. They got mad. That is when you looked and got mad too! That made me mad and hurt my feelings because I was the only one trying to work. Drip and Drop started the fight, but I am the only one who got in trouble, and they didn't even stick up for me. I am sorry I was loud, but I don't think it is fair I got in trouble.

If something happened with a classmate or teacher:
Are you proud of how you acted?
A little bit not

If not:
What can you do so that you are proud of yourself?
Maybe tell them

Be honest. Be brave. I believe in you!
Ms. Mary

"I'm really proud of you," she said.

"You are?!" **Drizzle** asked, astonished.

"Yep. It took a lot of courage to tell me you felt I was being unfair. Now that I know your side of the story, I think maybe I WAS being unfair. I'm sorry for assuming you were the only one making a poor choice."

"You are?!" **Drizzle** asked again.

"**Drizzle**, I was feeling frustrated that so much noise was coming from your table. It was distracting some of the other students. When I turned, I only saw you being loud, and so I assumed you were causing the problem," **Ms. Mary** explained.

"We can't help our feelings, **Drizzle**. It is important to feel them. HOW we deal with them is also important."

Drizzle looked at **Ms. Mary**. His shoulders drooped. "On my Raindrop Reflection I said I was a little not proud of my behavior."

"So what would you like to do about it?" she asked.

"I think I should apologize to **Drip** and **Drop**," he sighed.

> **MAKING CONNECTIONS**
>
> How are Ms. Mary and Drizzle alike?

"**Drip** and **Drop**, I was annoyed at you for fighting instead of just starting on our work.

But I'm sorry I yelled at you," he said with a catch in his voice.

And **Drip** and **Drop**? They told **Drizzle** they were sorry too – especially for letting him get in trouble when they were part of the problem.

It seemed like **Drizzle**'s day was ruined. He got in trouble for something he didn't do. Then he lost his temper and made the problem worse!

But he made it better. Even though giving his teacher that letter was one of the scariest things he'd ever done, he felt so much better afterwards. She was even proud of him for doing it!

You can't always control your feelings, but you CAN decide how to react to them.

And that's when doing the most difficult things can really pay off.

Getting in trouble is the WORST!

Especially when it's not your fault.

Draw a picture of a time YOU got in trouble and thought it was unfair.

NOW, **write a short story** telling us what happened. How did you solve the problem? Did you feel better afterwards?

_____

_____

_____

_____

_____

_____

_____

_____

_____

_____

Want more ideas like this one?
Visit Ms. Mary here for activities and challenges that regularly rotate!

CPSIA information can be obtained
at www.ICGtesting.com
Printed in the USA
BVHW022353031121
620554BV00023B/88